SCRAP REPUBLIC

8 QUILT PROJECTS FOR THOSE WHO LOVE COLOR

Emily Cier

C&T PUBLISHING

Text and Artwork copyright © 2011 by Emily Cier

Photography and Artwork copyright © 2011 by C&T Publishing, Inc.

Publisher: Amy Marson

Creative Director: Gailen Runge

Acquisitions Editor: Susanne Woods

Editor: Liz Aneloski

Technical Editors: Mary E. Flynn and Carolyn Aune

Cover Designer: Kristy Zacharias

Book Designer: April Mostek

Production Coordinator: Jenny Leicester

Production Editors: Julia Cianci and S. Michele Fry

Illustrator: Emily Cier

Quilt project photography by Christina Carty-Francis and Diane Pedersen of C&T Publishing, Inc.
Quilt art and how-to photos by Emily Cier.

Published by C&T Publishing, Inc., P.O. Box 1456, Lafayette, CA 94549

Library of Congress Cataloging-in-Publication Data

Cier, Emily.

 Scrap republic : 8 quilt projects for those who love color / Emily Cier.

   p. cm.

 ISBN 978-1-60705-214-2 (soft cover)

1. Patchwork quilts. 2. Quilting--Patterns. 3. Color in art. I. Title.

TT835.C4987 2011

746.46--dc22

2010054234

Printed in China

10 9 8 7 6 5 4 3 2

Acknowledgments

Sean | For being there for me every step of the way. He is truly the most quilt-literate software engineer ever who has never sewn a quilt (and he somewhat tolerates the overflowing scrap buckets too!).

Maeve and Liam | For oohing and aahing at all of Mommy's creations. The love you have for all your quilts makes my heart melt.

C&T Publishing | For all the creativity, hard work, and effort put forth by Amy, Gailen, Susanne, Liz, Mary, Carolyn, Kristy, April, Jenny, Julia and Michele. They helped make *Scrap Republic* rock!

Moda and Robert Kaufman | For providing fabulous fabrics for the print versions of these projects.

Contents

PROJECTS:

IMPORTANT
bits and pieces

Time to clear out the scrap buckets!

Gather and Sort Your Scraps

Get started by clearing out the hidden fabric stashes around your sewing room (and the rest of your house!). Find the following:

- Little stacks of fabric stuffed away that you swore you'd make into another quilt

- A single print from those beautiful collections of fabric you just knew you were going to buy more of in the future

- Pieces you'd cut out for a quilt but never finished

Put all of them into the scrap bucket.

Think of it as cleaning out your sewing room. Don't hold back. Do it. Throw it into the bucket!

Now it's time to sort.

I purchased ten large plastic buckets from my local super-store—one each for white, pink, red, orange, yellow, green, blue, purple, black/brown, and other. The "other" bucket was for random silks, flannels, denim, and bright multicolored prints. Fabrics in this bucket were not used in these projects.

I also made a pile of the larger scraps. Anything over ¼ yard went into this pile for use in the backing and binding.

Time to start sorting!

And just think how much room you'll have on your fabric shelves to go buy more fabric when you're done!

What color is it?

It's tough to figure out which bucket some prints belong in. Is it pink or red? Red or orange? Green or blue? The best way to sort these scraps is to hold the print in question next to both options and see which color it matches best. It's usually pretty clear after doing this, but if it isn't, then just put it aside for another project another day.

Are there too many colors in the print and you can't figure out what the main color is? Try squinting (or if you're like me, just take your glasses off). Squinting removes the details, and the main color will pop out.

Some prints are just too busy for these projects. Put those into your "other" bucket for a future project.

Piecing Ideas

Each project includes piecing instructions for making a quilt like the one shown. The beauty of these projects is that there are many other ways to piece the scrap blocks, and each would yield a completely different quilt.

Some alternate scrap-piecing ideas:

If you do not have large enough scraps for any of the pieces needed, piece smaller scraps together and then trim to the right size.

How do you take these ideas and translate them into a different quilt?

Let's take *Volume* (page 34) as an example. This time we're going to make it with the idea shown in the blue block on the previous page. I hope you're inspired by the possibilities.

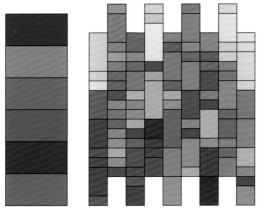

Original block and quilt

Starburst block and quilt

Thread Scraps

These quilts are a great way to use up the countless bobbins with only a small amount of thread remaining. Let's face it—thread is expensive. Use up the bobbins as your top or bobbin thread.

Backing Ideas

Piecing your backing can be both economical and a great way to use up those pesky ½- to 1-yard cuts that are left after other projects.

For the smaller quilts, piecing isn't always necessary, and you can use large 1-yard cuts.

The backing print designs can relate to the quilting design or the quilt top.

Don't have any scraps large-enough to use for the backing? Try simple and inexpensive solids that match the look and feel of your quilt top.

Layering and Basting

Spread the backing wrong side up and tape the edges down with masking tape. (If you are working on carpet, you can use T-pins to secure the backing to the carpet.) Center the batting on top, smoothing out any folds. Place the quilt top right side up on top of the batting and backing, making sure it is centered.

If you plan to machine quilt, pin baste the quilt layers together with safety pins placed a minimum of 3"–4" apart. Begin basting in the center and move toward the edges first in vertical, then horizontal, rows. Try not to pin directly on the intended quilting lines.

If you plan to hand quilt, baste the layers together with thread using a long needle and light-colored thread. Knot one end of the thread. Using stitches approximately the length of the needle, begin in the center and move out toward the edges in vertical and horizontal rows approximately 4" apart. Add two diagonal rows of basting.

Quilting Ideas

When it comes to quilting, try to incorporate the lines and texture created by the scraps into the quilting design. This will make both the prints and the quilting pop. You can use the quilting to emphasize shapes in the quilt and separate one color from another or the background from the colors.

Some other quilting ideas:

Parallel lines

Stippling

Circles

Lattice

Longarm pantograph

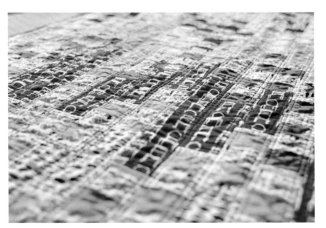

Echo

Uneven parallel lines

Binding

Each project includes measurements for binding from either scraps or yardage. I chose to use larger ⅜- to ⅝-yard scraps in order to have a single print for my binding, but you can also use several scrap strips pieced together.

Trim excess batting and backing from the quilt even with the edges of the quilt top.

Double-Fold Straight-Grain Binding

If you want a ¼" finished binding, cut the binding strips 2½" wide and piece them together with diagonal seams to make a continuous binding strip. Trim the seam allowance to ¼". Press the seams open.

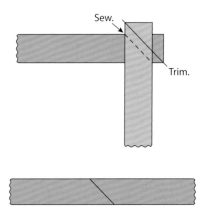

Press the entire strip in half lengthwise with wrong sides together. With raw edges even, pin the binding to the front edge of the quilt a few inches away from the corner, and leave the first few inches of the binding unattached.

1. Start sewing, using a ¼" seam allowance. Stop ¼" away from the first corner; backstitch one stitch.

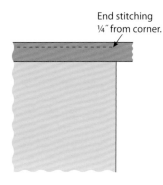

2. Lift the presser foot and needle. Rotate the quilt one-quarter turn. Fold the binding at a right angle so it extends straight above the quilt and the fold forms a 45° angle in the corner.

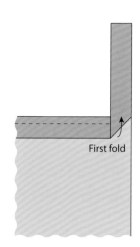

3. Then bring the binding strip down even with the edge of the quilt. Begin sewing at the folded edge. Repeat in the same manner at all corners.

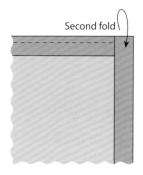

4. Continue stitching until you are back near the beginning of the binding strip.

Finishing the Binding Ends

METHOD 1

1. After stitching around the quilt, fold under the beginning tail of the binding strip ¼" so that the raw edge will be inside the binding after it is turned to the back of the quilt.

2. Place the end tail of the binding strip over the beginning folded end. Continue to attach the binding and stitch slightly beyond the starting stitches. Trim the excess binding.

3. Fold the binding over the raw edges to the quilt back and hand stitch, mitering the corners.

METHOD 2

(See our blog entry at ctpubblog.com; search for *invisible seam* and then scroll down to Quilting Tips: Completing a Binding with an Invisible Seam.)

1. Fold the ending tail of the binding back on itself where it meets the beginning binding tail. From the fold, measure and mark the cut width of your binding strip. Cut the ending binding tail to this measurement. For example, if your binding is cut 2½" wide, measure from the fold on the ending tail of the binding 2½" and cut the binding tail to this length.

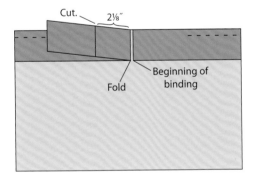

Cut. 2⅛"

Fold Beginning of binding

2. Open both tails. Place one tail on top of the other tail at right angles, right sides together. Mark a diagonal line from corner to corner and stitch on the line. Check that you've done it correctly and that the binding fits the quilt; then trim the seam allowance to ¼". Press open.

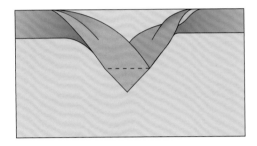

3. Refold the binding and stitch this binding section in place on the quilt. Fold the binding over the raw edges to the quilt back and hand stitch.

Don't Have Enough Scraps?

If you don't have enough scraps for a project, here are some ways to expand your scrap bucket empire:

- Make the print versions of the project quilts first. Each project in this book includes instructions on how to make the same pattern with yardage straight from your favorite local or online quilt shop. More quilts = more scraps!

- Buy my first book, *Quilt Remix*, and make those projects. Before you know it, you'll have more scraps than you know what to do with!

- Use fat quarters. These are an easy and inexpensive way to bulk up specific color groups.

- Check out your local quilt shop or Etsy. Many shops and crafters sell their scraps.

- Take some of mine. I was hoping that writing this book would finally deplete my scrap stash. It didn't even make a dent. My husband would greatly appreciate it if someone would remove my scrap buckets. I can't bring myself to listen to my own advice.

Be eccentric. Be crazy. And most important, *have fun*! It's very liberating!

Freckles

Plumb

Beeline

Slices

Small and simple projects if you:

- are a beginner;

- don't have huge scrap stashes (*yet*, but you are working daily toward alleviating this problem); or

- are looking for a quick or small project.

FRECKLES

Freckles in Scraps, pieced and quilted by Emily Cier, 30" × 30"

SCRAP SELECTION

The background of the quilt can be a single piece of a light neutral fabric or pieced from scraps with little contrast.

The dots should vary in color, ranging from light pink to black. They can be pieced or single pieces of fabric. Feel free to fussy cut particular designs from your scraps.

Make sure you have significant contrast between the background fabric and the dots.

what you need

* Light neutral large scraps for background

* Pink, red, orange, yellow, green, blue, purple, brown, and black small scraps to piece together for dots

* Backing: Pieced to 39″ × 39″ *or* 1⅛ yards

* Batting: 39″ × 39″

* Binding: 2½″ wide × 140″ long, pieced from scraps; *or* ⅜ yard (cut into 4 strips)

ASSEMBLY

1. Sew the neutral scraps for the background together to measure slightly larger than 30½″ × 30½″, and then trim to 30½″ × 30½″.

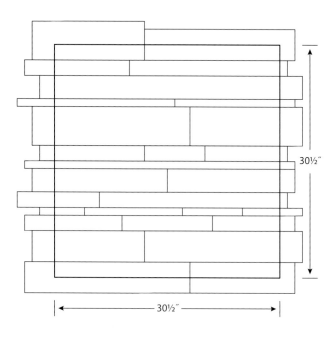

30½″

30½″

2. Piece and press the small scraps together to make pieces large enough to cut out the dots (a circle rotary cutter can help with this: www.olfa.com) measuring 3″ finished. For alternate piecing designs, see Piecing Ideas (page 7).

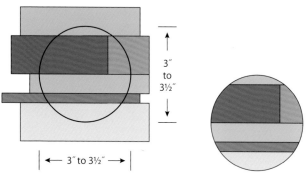

3″ to 3½″

← 3″ to 3½″ →

note

If you are using turn-under appliqué, be sure to add your preferred seam allowance. For raw-edge appliqué, cut to the finished size.

Pink: Cut 3.	**Yellow:** Cut 2.	**Purple:** Cut 3.
Red: Cut 2.	**Green:** Cut 5.	**Brown:** Cut 1.
Orange: Cut 3.	**Blue:** Cut 5.	**Black:** Cut 1.

note

I arranged the rows of dots from light to dark within color families.

3. Arrange the circles on the background and baste or pin them in place. Appliqué the circles onto the background fabric, using your favorite method.

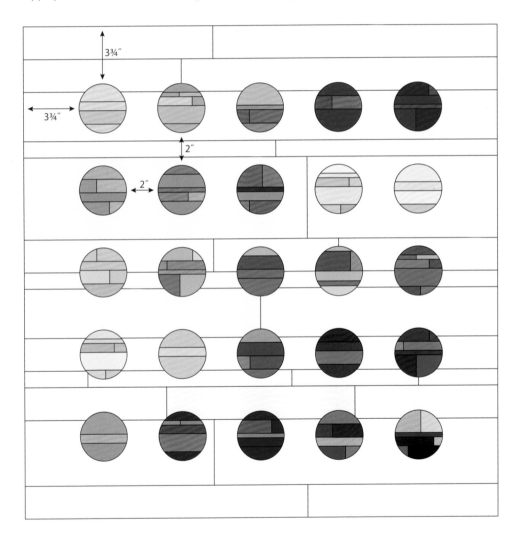

FINISHING

Layer, quilt, and bind (Layering and Basting, Quilting Ideas, and Binding, pages 9–13).

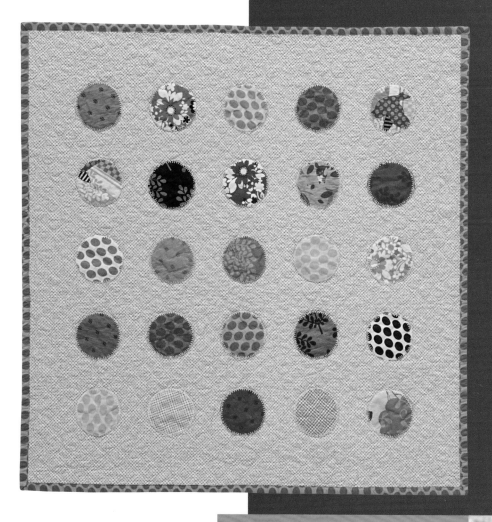

SOLACE FOR THE SCRAPLESS

Trim following Step 2 on page 17.

Place dots and assemble following Step 3 on page 18.

For this version of *Freckles*, use yardage rather than scraps.

- ◆ Background: 1 yard trimmed to 30½″ × 30½″

- ◆ Dots: 25 charm squares (5″ × 5″)

PLUMB

Plumb in Scraps, pieced and quilted by Emily Cier, 30″ × 30″

what you need

- Red, orange, yellow, green, blue, and purple scraps (at least 1″–2″ wide and 5″ long)

- White scraps (long, skinny pieces) for borders

- Backing: Pieced to 39″ × 39″ *or* 1⅛ yards

- Batting: 39″ × 39″

- Binding: 2½″ wide × 140″ long, pieced from scraps; *or* ⅜ yard (cut into 4 strips)

SCRAP SELECTION

Gather the scraps you'll be using for each color strip and roughly arrange them from lightest to darkest. Sew the scraps into 3 or 4 sections and check the length, adding a few more scraps if necessary before sewing the final seams to complete the color block.

ASSEMBLY

1. Piece the borders slightly oversized, then trim and press to make 2 side strips 3½″ × 24½″ and 2 top/bottom strips 3½″ × 30½″.

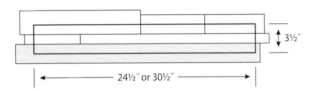

2. Find colored scraps that are about 1″ × 2″wide and about 5″ long (or cut larger scraps down to these dimensions). Roughly arrange the scraps of each of the 6 colors from lightest to darkest. Sew each color into a strip slightly larger than 4½″ × 24½″. Press. Trim each of the 6 strips to 4½″ × 24½″.

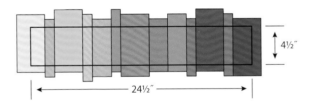

For alternate piecing designs, see Piecing Ideas (page 7).

3. Sew the 6 color strips together.

4. Sew the side borders (3½″ × 24½″) onto the quilt top. Add the top and bottom borders (3½″ × 30½″).

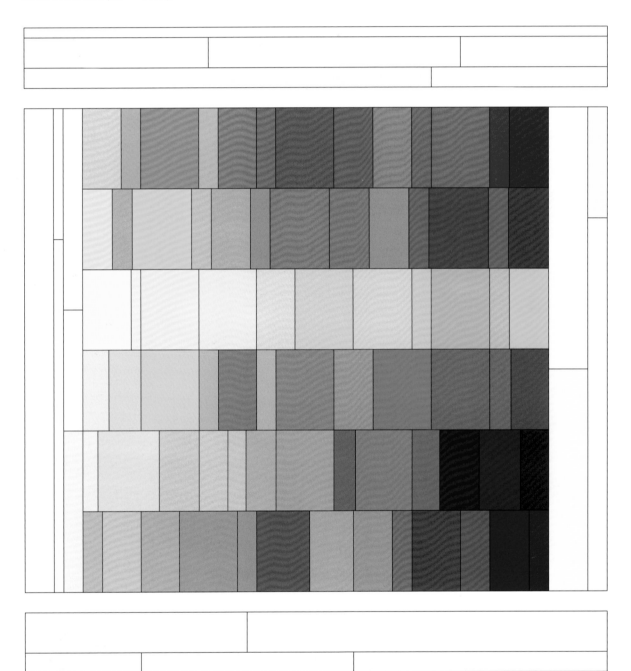

FINISHING

Layer, quilt, and bind (Layering and Basting, Quilting Ideas, and Binding, pages 9–13).

Plumb in Prints, pieced and quilted by Emily Cier, 30″ × 30″

SOLACE FOR THE SCRAPLESS

Trim charm squares to widths varying from 1″–5″.

Stitch trimmed "scraps" into 6 strips just over 24½″ long. You can separate color families like in the example shown, or you can go for a scrappier, more random look. Trim each strip to 4½″ × 24½″.

Cut border fabric to make 2 side strips 3½″ × 24½″ and 2 top/bottom strips 3½″ × 30½″.

Complete assembly by following Steps 3 and 4 on page 22.

For this version of *Plumb*, use yardage rather than scraps.

- ◆ Stripes: 2 packs of charm squares

- ◆ Borders: ½ yard

BEELINE

what you need

- White scraps (long, skinny pieces) for borders

- Red, orange, yellow, green, blue, and purple scraps (2″–3″ wide × 3″–25″ long)

- Backing: Pieced to 39″ × 39″ *or* 1⅛ yards

- Batting: 39″ × 39″

- Binding: 2½″ wide × 140″ long, pieced from scraps; *or* ⅜ yard (cut into 4 strips)

SCRAP SELECTION

This quilt's long pieces give you the opportunity to use some of your larger scraps and scraps with big prints. Binding strips left over from other projects work well. Make sure the prints don't have too much contrast within them as you may end up losing the main color. If you don't have long enough scraps, piece smaller scraps together to form the finished unit.

ASSEMBLY

1. Piece the borders slightly oversize and trim to make 2 side strips 3½″ × 24½″ and 2 top/bottom strips 3½″ × 30½″.

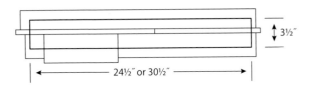

2. Piece the scraps into oversized strips; press. Trim the red, orange, green, and purple scraps each into 2 strips 1½″ × 24½″ and 1 strip 2½″ × 24½″. Trim the yellow scraps into 4 strips 1½″ × 24½″. Trim the blue scraps into 2 strips 2½″ × 24½″.

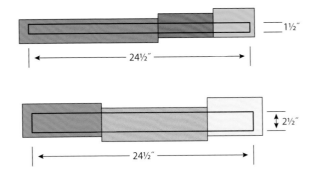

For alternate piecing designs, see Piecing Ideas (page 7).

3. Sew the colored strips together.

4. Sew the side borders (24½″ × 3½″) onto the quilt top. Add the top and bottom borders (30½″ × 3½″).

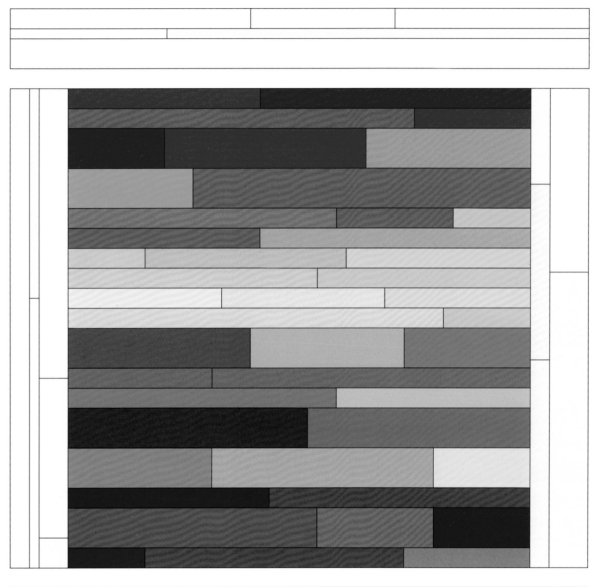

FINISHING

Layer, quilt, and bind (Layering and Basting, Quilting Ideas, and Binding, pages 9–13).

Beeline in Prints, pieced and quilted by Emily Cier, 30″ × 30″

SOLACE FOR THE SCRAPLESS

For stripes, cut each print into 2 strips 1½″ × 24½″ and 1 strip 2½″ × 24½″

Assign each print a letter, A through F, and assemble as shown.

For borders, cut the fabric into 2 side strips 3½″ × 24½″ and 2 top/bottom strips 3½″ × 30½″

Add following Step 4 on page 26.

For this version of *Beeline*, use yardage rather than scraps.

- ◆ Stripes: ¼ yard each of 6 prints

- ◆ Borders: ½ yard

| A |
| B |
| C |
| D |

| A |
| E |
| F |
| B |
| C |
| D |
| E |
| F |
| C |
| B |
| F |
| E |
| A |
| D |

SLICES

Slices in Scraps, pieced and quilted by Emily Cier, 30″ × 30″

what you need

- White, pink, red, orange, yellow, green, blue, and purple scraps (1″–3″ wide × 3″–10″ long)

- Backing: Pieced to 39″ × 39″ *or* 1⅛ yards

- Batting: 39″ × 39″

- Binding: 2½″ wide × 140″ long, pieced from scraps; *or* ⅜ yard (cut into 4 strips)

SCRAP SELECTION

For added effect, use lighter colors at the top tip of each triangle and darker colors at the base. This is a good pattern for using up a variety of widths of scraps as well: narrow at the top and wider at the bottom.

ASSEMBLY

1. Sew the scraps for Triangles A, A-reverse, and B into units slightly larger than the dimensions listed below. Make the quantity listed in Step 2.

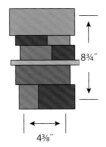

Use for Triangle A and A-reverse

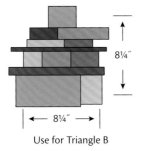

Use for Triangle B

For alternate piecing designs, see Piecing Ideas (page 7).

2. Press and trim to the rough size.

White:

2 rectangles 4⅜″ × 8¾″
(Trim 1 to A; trim 1 to A-reverse. Refer to Step 3 on page 30.)

3 squares 8¼″ × 8¼″
(Trim to B. Refer to Step 4 on page 30.)

Pink:

4 squares 8¼″ × 8¼″
(Trim to B.)

Red:

4 squares 8¼″ × 8¼″
(Trim to B.)

Orange:

2 rectangles 4⅜″ × 8¾″
(Trim 1 to A; trim 1 to A-reverse.)

3 squares 8¼″ × 8¼″
(Trim to B.)

Yellow:

2 rectangles 4⅜″ × 8¾″
(Trim 1 to A; trim 1 to A-reverse.)

3 squares 8¼″ × 8¼″
(Trim to B.)

Green:

4 squares 8¼″ × 8¼″
(Trim to B.)

Blue:

4 squares 8¼″ × 8¼″
(Trim to B.)

Purple:

2 rectangles 4⅜″ × 8¾″
(Trim 1 to A; trim 1 to A-reverse.)

3 squares 8¼″ × 8¼″
(Trim to B.)

3. Stack 2 pieced 4⅜″ × 8¾″ rectangles with the wrong sides together and cut out A and its reverse (A-reverse) triangles at the same time. Refer to Step 2 for the quantity of each color to cut.

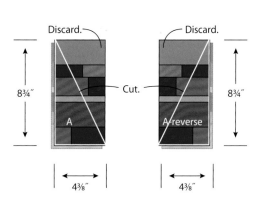

Discard. — Cut. — Discard.

8¾″

A   A-reverse

8¾″

4⅜″   4⅜″

4. Cut out the B pieces from the 8¼″ squares. Refer to Step 2 for the quantity of each color to cut.

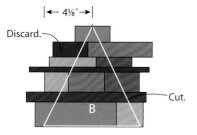

|← 4⅛″ →|

Discard.

Cut.

B

5. Sew the triangles into 4 rows and then sew the 4 rows together.

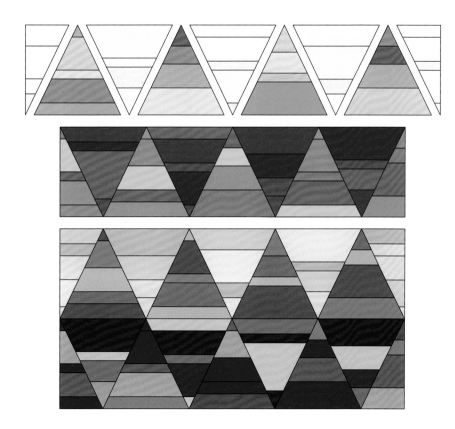

TIP

* When you sew Triangles A and A-reverse to Triangle B, it may seem as if the shapes won't fit, but the seamlines are the right size. After stitching, you'll get "bunny ears."

* Starching the fabric first helps you maintain control of the bias edges.

FINISHING

Layer, quilt, and bind (Layering and Basting, Quilting Ideas, and Binding, pages 9–13).

SOLACE FOR THE SCRAPLESS

White:

Cut 1 strip 8¾" × width of fabric (wof) from each white print; subcut each strip into 2 rectangles 4⅜" × 8¾"

(Trim 2 to A; trim 2 to A-reverse.)

Trim strip remainders to 8¼" and subcut into 2 squares 8¼" × 8¼".

(Trim to B.)

Blue:

Cut 1 strip 8¼" × wof; subcut into 4 squares 8¼" × 8¼".

(Trim to B.)

Red:

Cut 1 strip 8¾" × wof from each red print; subcut each strip into 2 rectangles 4⅜" × 8¾".

(Trim 1 of each print to A; trim 1 of each print to A-reverse.)

Trim strip remainders to 8¼" and subcut into 3 squares 8¼" × 8¼".

(Trim to B.)

Brown:

Cut 1 strip 8¼" × wof from each brown print; subcut each strip into 4 squares 8¼" × 8¼".

(Trim to B.)

Pink:

Cut 1 strip 8¼" × wof from each pink print; subcut into 3 squares 8¼" × 8¼".

(Trim to B.)

Assemble following Step 5 on page 30.

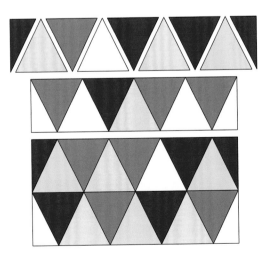

Slices in Prints, pieced and quilted by Emily Cier, 30" × 30"

For this version of *Slices*, use yardage rather than scraps.

White: 2 prints, ¼ yard each

Blue: 1 print, ¼ yard

Red: 2 prints, ¼ yard each

Brown: 2 prints, ¼ yard each

Pink: 2 prints, ¼ yard each

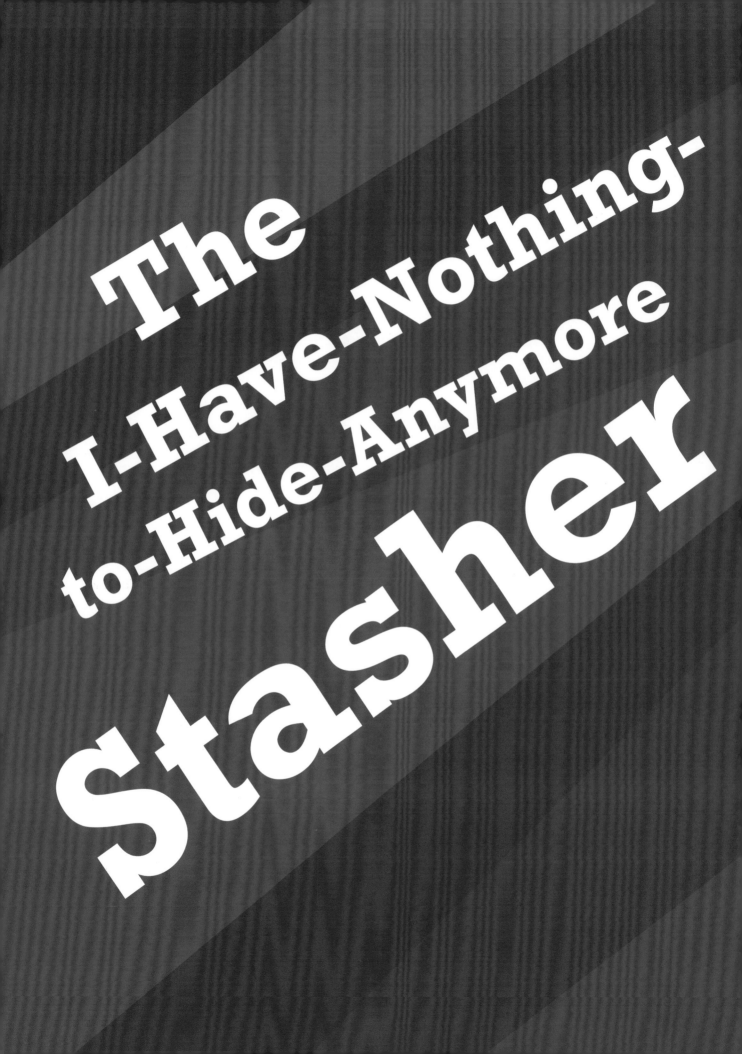

Volume

Hover

Whirl

Pivot

Larger quilts and more complex projects if you:

- no longer care how much fabric you've really collected and are so proud of it that no one dares to commit you to Fabric Stashers Anonymous;

- happily share the dining room table and nightly dinners with your favorite prints, but aren't so off the deep end that you talk to them (yet);

- are considering finishing your attic to hide the goods;

- feel like Norm walking into Cheers when visiting your local quilt shops—yes, everyone knows your name;

- have a stash that grows by the day (aided by your daily trip to the quilt shop); or

- save every scrap, yet deny everything when quizzed by your children about the tiny pieces of fabric they find stashed in their backpacks.

VOLUME

Volume in Scraps, pieced and quilted by Emily Cier, 40" × 48"

what you need

- White, pink, red, orange, yellow, green, blue, purple, and brown/black scraps (3″ × lengths no more than 7″; 1″–2″ recommended)

- Backing: Pieced to 48″ × 56″ *or* 3⅛ yards

- Batting: 48″ × 56″

- Binding: 2½″ wide × 196″ long, pieced from scraps; *or* ½ yard (cut into 5 strips)

SCRAP SELECTION

While you can always cut smaller pieces from large scraps, this is a great quilt for using up all your tiny scraps. A large majority of the pieces I used in the quilt measured less than 2″ × 3″. Smaller prints without much contrast work best. For a gradated look, make light, medium, and dark blocks for each color, putting the lighter colors toward the left and the darker colors toward the right.

ASSEMBLY

1. Find (or cut) scraps of various lengths approximately 3″ wide.

2. Sew these pieces into units slightly larger than the dimensions listed in Step 3. Make the quantity listed.

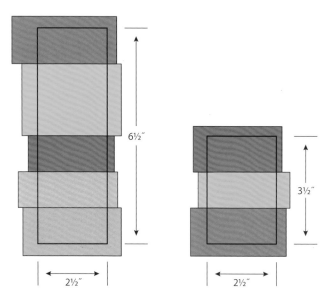

For alternate piecing designs, see Piecing Ideas (page 7).

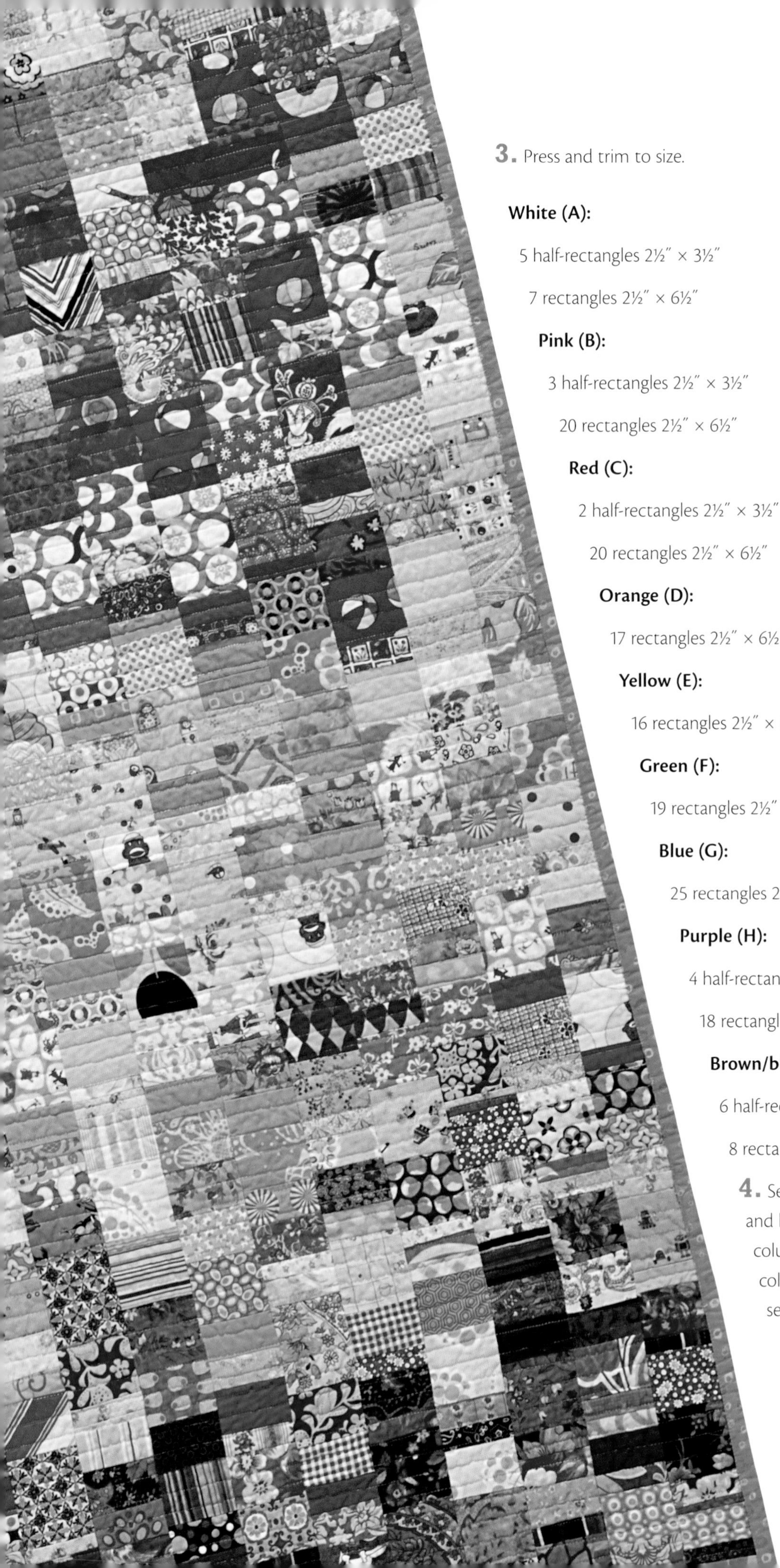

3. Press and trim to size.

White (A):

5 half-rectangles 2½″ × 3½″

7 rectangles 2½″ × 6½″

Pink (B):

3 half-rectangles 2½″ × 3½″

20 rectangles 2½″ × 6½″

Red (C):

2 half-rectangles 2½″ × 3½″

20 rectangles 2½″ × 6½″

Orange (D):

17 rectangles 2½″ × 6½″

Yellow (E):

16 rectangles 2½″ × 6½″

Green (F):

19 rectangles 2½″ × 6½″

Blue (G):

25 rectangles 2½″ × 6½″

Purple (H):

4 half-rectangles 2½″ × 3½″

18 rectangles 2½″ × 6½″

Brown/black (I):

6 half-rectangles 2½″ × 3½″

8 rectangles 2½″ × 6½″

4. Sew the rectangles (2½″ × 6½″) and half-rectangles (2½″ × 3½″) into columns as shown and then sew the columns together. Press the column seams open to reduce bulk.

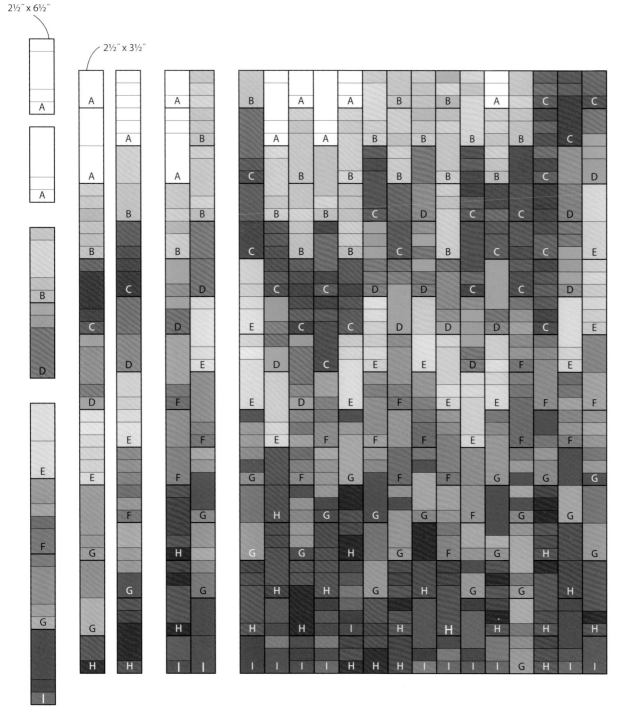

2½″ x 6½″

2½″ x 3½″

FINISHING

Layer, quilt, and bind (Layering and Basting, Quilting Ideas, and Binding, pages 9–13).

Volume in Prints, pieced and quilted by Emily Cier, 40″ × 48″

For this version of *Volume*, use yardage rather than scraps.

A: ¼ yard

B: ⅜ yard

C: ⅜ yard

D: ⅓ yard

E: ⅓ yard

F: ⅜ yard

G: ½ yard

H: ⅜ yard

I: ¼ yard

SOLACE FOR THE SCRAPLESS

A: Cut 2 strips 2½″ × width of fabric (wof); subcut into:

5 half-rectangles 2½″ × 3½″

7 rectangles 2½″ × 6½″

B: Cut 4 strips 2½″ × wof; subcut into:

3 half-rectangles 2½″ × 3½″

20 rectangles 2½″ × 6½″

C: Cut 4 strips 2½″ × wof; subcut into:

2 half-rectangles 2½″ × 3½″

20 rectangles 2½″ × 6½″

D: Cut 3 strips 2½″ × wof; subcut into:

17 rectangles 2½″ × 6½″

E: Cut 3 strips 2½″ × wof; subcut into:

16 rectangles 2½″ × 6½″

F: Cut 4 strips 2½″ × wof; subcut into:

19 rectangles 2½″ × 6½″

G: Cut 5 strips 2½″ × wof; subcut into:

25 rectangles 2½″ × 6½″

H: Cut 4 strips 2½″ × wof; subcut into:

4 half-rectangles 2½″ × 3½″

18 rectangles 2½″ × 6½″

I: Cut 2 strips 2½″ × wof; subcut into:

6 half-rectangles 2½″ × 3½″

8 rectangles 2½″ × 6½″

Assemble the half-rectangles and rectangles following Step 4 on page 36.

HOVER

Hover in Scraps, pieced and quilted by Emily Cier, 48" × 48"

SCRAP SELECTION

You can choose whether to have a single print per colored loop (or round) or different prints in the same color for each piece of the loop. I opted to use different prints. If you pick this option, try to avoid particularly light or dark prints so that you end up with a cohesive loop of color.

what you need

- White, pink, red, orange, yellow, green, blue, and purple scraps (various sizes; see chart below.)

- Backing: Pieced to 56″ × 56″ *or* 3⅛ yards

- Batting: 56″ × 56″

- Binding: 2½″ wide × 212″ long, pieced from scraps; *or* ½ yard (cut into 6 strips)

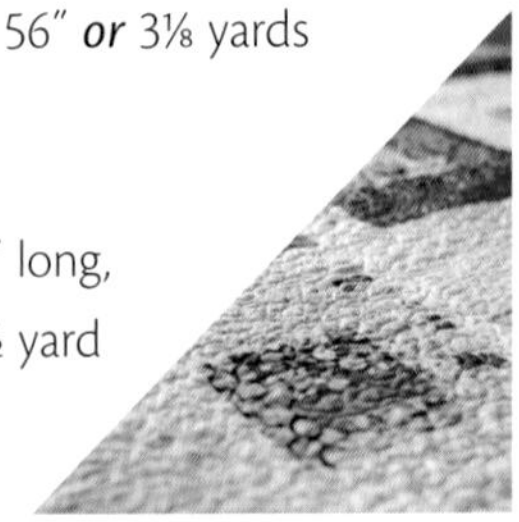

ASSEMBLY

Finished block size: 12″ × 12″

1. Using the chart below, trim scraps to the following sizes.

	WHITE	PINK	RED	ORANGE	YELLOW	GREEN	BLUE	PURPLE
1½″ × 1½″			3		5		1	3
1½″ × 2½″		6	1		2	3	6	
1½″ × 3½″		5	3	3	4	2	5	2
1½″ × 4½″		1	2	2		1	6	
1½″ × 5½″					1		1	2
1½″ × 6½″				2			2	4
1½″ × 7½″	4	2		2	1	2	1	4
1½″ × 8½″		3		4	1	1	1	2
1½″ × 9½″	4	2		4				2
1½″ × 10½″	8							
1½″ × 12½″	24							
2½″ × 2½″			2		1		1	
2½″ × 3½″			3	1		4	4	
2½″ × 4½″		3		2		3	2	2
2½″ × 5½″		2			3	2	3	2
2½″ × 7½″			2		1	4	3	2
2½″ × 9½″				2			2	4
2½″ × 10½″	8							
2½″ × 12½″	4							
3½″ × 8½″		1			1	1	1	
3½″ × 9½″	4							
4½″ × 7½″	4							
4½″ × 12½″	4							

All the blocks are assembled in the same manner—loop by loop (or round by round)—but the measurements vary. You will build four of each block, but the colors will vary. Specific instructions for each block are on pages 42–43. Press all seam allowances to the outside. Cut sizes are shown in the diagrams.

2. Sew the shorter Loop 2 strips to the top and bottom of the center, Loop 1. Press. Sew the longer Loop 2 strips to the left and right sides. Press.

3. Sew the shorter Loop 3 strips to the top and bottom of the unit from the previous step. Press. Sew the longer Loop 3 strips to the left and right sides. Press.

4. Continue sewing the loops according to each block diagram, starting with the shorter strips on the top and bottom, pressing, and then sewing the longer strips on the left and right sides and pressing.

5. Using the illustration and chart for each block, make 4 blocks for each letter. Follow the charts on the next pages for the correct color combinations.

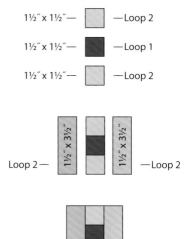

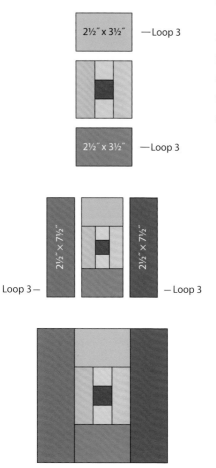

Block A

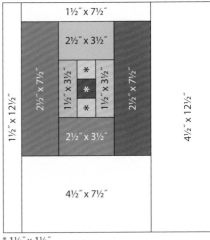

1½" x 7½"
2½" x 3½"
1½" x 3½"
1½" x 3½"
2½" x 7½"
2½" x 7½"
1½" x 12½"
4½" x 12½"
2½" x 3½"
4½" x 7½"

* 1½" x 1½"

In the following charts, the colors refer to *Hover in Scraps* and the letters (A)–(H) refer to the corresponding fabrics in *Hover in Prints*.

Block	A1	A2	A3	A4
Loop 1	red (C)	yellow (E)	blue (G)	purple (H)
Loop 2	yellow (E)	purple (H)	red (C)	yellow (E)
Loop 3	green (F)	blue (G)	green (F)	red (C)
Loop 4	white (A)	white (A)	white (A)	white (A)

Block B

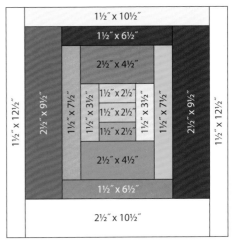

1½" x 10½"
1½" x 6½"
2½" x 4½"
1½" x 2½"
2½" x 9½"
1½" x 7½"
1½" x 3½"
1½" x 2½"
1½" x 3½"
1½" x 7½"
2½" x 9½"
1½" x 12½"
1½" x 2½"
1½" x 12½"
2½" x 4½"
1½" x 6½"
2½" x 10½"

Block	B1	B2	B3	B4
Loop 1	yellow (E)	green (F)	red (C)	yellow (E)
Loop 2	pink (B)	blue (G)	pink (B)	green (F)
Loop 3	orange (D)	purple (H)	green (F)	pink (B)
Loop 4	purple (H)	orange (D)	purple (H)	blue (G)
Loop 5	white (A)	white (A)	white (A)	white (A)

Block C

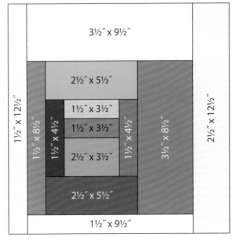

3½" x 9½"
2½" x 5½"
1½" x 3½"
1½" x 8½"
1½" x 4½"
1½" x 3½"
1½" x 4½"
1½" x 12½"
2½" x 3½"
3½" x 8½"
2½" x 12½"
2½" x 5½"
1½" x 9½"

Block	C1	C2	C3	C4
Loop 1	orange (D)	pink (B)	orange (D)	blue (G)
Loop 2	blue (G)	red (C)	blue (G)	orange (D)
Loop 3	green (F)	blue (G)	yellow (E)	pink (B)
Loop 4	white (A)	white (A)	white (A)	white (A)

Block D

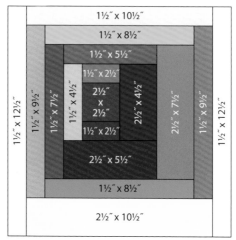

Block	D1	D2	D3	D4
Loop 1	red (C)	blue (G)	yellow (F)	red (C)
Loop 2	blue (G)	green (F)	pink (B)	blue (G)
Loop 3	purple (H)	yellow (E)	blue (G)	purple (H)
Loop 4	orange (D)	pink (B)	purple (H)	orange (D)
Loop 5	white (A)	white (A)	white (A)	white (A)

6. Following the diagram below, sew the blocks into a completed quilt top. Press. Take note of the rotations in the squares.

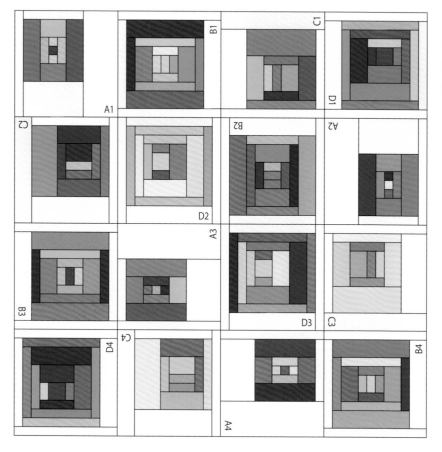

FINISHING

Layer, quilt, and bind (Layering and Basting, Quilting Ideas, and Binding, pages 9–13).

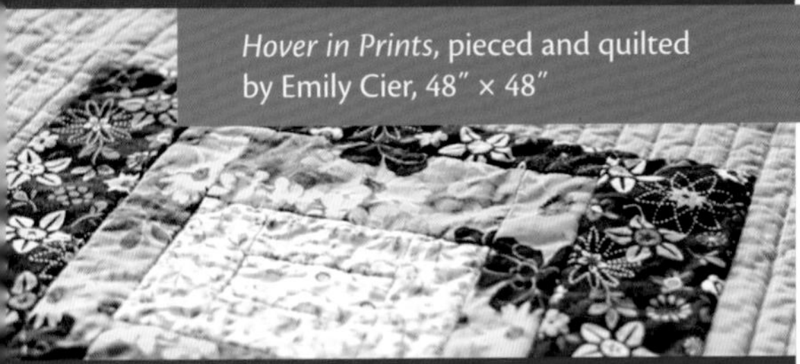

Hover in Prints, pieced and quilted by Emily Cier, 48″ × 48″

For this version of *Hover*, use yardage rather than scraps.

A: 1½ yards

B: ½ yard

C: ¼ yard

D: ⅜ yard

E: ⅜ yard

F: ½ yard

G: ⅝ yard

H: ½ yard

SOLACE FOR THE SCRAPLESS

Print	FIRST CUT Quantity	FIRST CUT Dimensions*	SECOND CUT Quantity	SECOND CUT Dimensions
A	13	1½″ × wof	4	1½″ × 7½″
			4	1½″ × 9½″
			8	1½″ × 10½″
			24	1½″ × 12½″
	4	2½″ × wof	8	2½″ × 10½″
			4	2½″ × 12½″
	1	3½″ × wof	4	3½″ × 9½″
	3	4½″ × wof	4	4½″ × 7½″
			4	4½″ × 12½″
B	3	1½″ × wof	6	1½″ × 2½″
			5	1½″ × 3½″
			1	1½″ × 4½″
			2	1½″ × 7½″
			3	1½″ × 8½″
			2	1½″ × 9½″
	1	2½″ × wof	3	2½″ × 4½″
			2	2½″ × 5½″
	1	3½″ × wof	1	3½″ × 8½″
C	1	1½″ × wof	3	1½″ × 1½″
			1	1½″ × 2½″
			3	1½″ × 3½″
			2	1½″ × 4½″
	1	2½″ × wof	2	2½″ × 2½″
			3	2½″ × 3½″
			2	2½″ × 7½″

* *wof = width of fabric*

Assemble the blocks by referring to Steps 2–5 on page 41 and the corresponding block charts on pages 42–43.

Print	FIRST CUT		SECOND CUT	
	Quantity	Dimensions*	Quantity	Dimensions
D	4	1½″ × wof	3	1½″ × 3½″
			2	1½″ × 4½″
			2	1½″ × 6½″
			2	1½″ × 7½″
			4	1½″ × 8½″
			4	1½″ × 9½″
	1	2½″ × wof	1	2½″ × 3½″
			2	2½″ × 4½″
			2	2½″ × 9½″
E	2	1½″ × wof	5	1½″ × 1½″
			2	1½″ × 2½″
			4	1½″ × 3½″
			1	1½″ × 5½″
			1	1½″ × 7½″
			1	1½″ × 8½″
	1	2½″ × wof	1	2½″ × 2½″
			3	2½″ × 5½″
			1	2½″ × 7½″
	1	3½″ × wof	1	3½″ × 8½″
F	2	1½″ × wof	5	1½″ × 2½″
			2	1½″ × 3½″
			1	1½″ × 4½″
			2	1½″ × 7½″
			1	1½″ × 8½″
	2	2½″ × wof	4	2½″ × 3½″
			3	2½″ × 4½″
			2	2½″ × 5½″
			4	2½″ × 7½″
	1	3½″ × wof	1	3½″ × 8½″

Print	FIRST CUT		SECOND CUT	
	Quantity	Dimensions*	Quantity	Dimensions
G	3	1½″ × wof	1	1½″ × 1½″
			6	1½″ × 2½″
			5	1½″ × 3½″
			6	1½″ × 4½″
			1	1½″ × 5½″
			2	1½″ × 6½″
			1	1½″ × 7½″
			1	1½″ × 8½″
	3	2½″ × wof	1	2½″ × 2½″
			4	2½″ × 3½″
			2	2½″ × 4½″
			3	2½″ × 5½″
			3	2½″ × 7½″
			2	2½″ × 9½″
	1	3½″ × wof	1	3½″ × 8½″
H	4	1½″ × wof	3	1½″ × 1½″
			2	1½″ × 3½″
			2	1½″ × 5½″
			4	1½″ × 6½″
			4	1½″ × 7½″
			2	1½″ × 8½″
			2	1½″ × 9½″
	2	2½″ × wof	2	2½″ × 4½″
			2	2½″ × 5½″
			2	2½″ × 7½″
			4	2½″ × 9½″

WHIRL

Whirl in Scraps, pieced by Emily Cier, quilted by Cathy Kirk, 64″ × 64″

SCRAP SELECTION

I used skinny strips placed at a 45° angle to make this quilt. The skinny strips gave the finished quilt lots of texture, and the angle added movement and a subtle lattice effect.

ASSEMBLY

Finished block size: 4″ × 4″

1. Piece together scraps to form roughly 5½″ squares. Press and trim down to 5⅛″ squares in the following quantities:

Pink: Cut 34.   **Green:** Cut 31.

Red: Cut 36.   **Blue:** Cut 49.

Orange: Cut 45.   **Purple:** Cut 47.

Yellow: Cut 17.

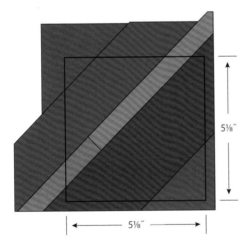

For alternate piecing designs, see Piecing Ideas (page 7).

what you need

◆ Pink, red, orange, yellow, green, blue, and purple scraps (3″–9″ × 1″–3″)

◆ Backing: Pieced to 72″ × 72″ *or* 4 yards

◆ Batting: 72″ × 72″

◆ Binding: 2½″ wide × 280″ long, pieced from scraps; *or* ⅝ yard (cut into 7 strips)

2. Using Templates 1 and 2, cut 1 outer (1) and 1 inner (2) piece from each square.

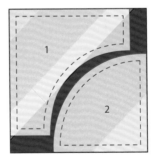

3. Sew a 1 piece and a 2 piece together in the combinations and quantities listed in the chart on page 48. (You will have a few 1 pieces and a few 2 pieces left over when you are done.)

The colors refer to the scrap colors in *Whirl in Scraps*, the letters (A)–(G) refer to the corresponding prints in *Whirl in Prints*.

		TEMPLATE 2 (INNER PIECE)						
		pink (A)	red (B)	orange (C)	yellow (D)	green (E)	blue (F)	purple (G)
TEMPLATE 1 (OUTER PIECE)	pink (A)						13	20
	red (B)					2	17	17
	orange (C)		2	1	1	19	14	8
	yellow (D)			1		8	4	2
	green (E)	1	3	17	9	1		
	blue (F)	10	15	17	6	1		
	purple (G)	23	15	8	1			

4. Fold pieces 1 and 2 in half as shown and crease at seamline.

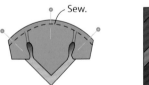

Fold and crease.

Fold and crease.

5. Layer 1 and 2, right sides together, with A on top. Align the center creases and pin.

6. Align the corners of 1 and 2 on the left side and pin. Repeat on the right side.

> **TIP**
>
> * If you are unfamiliar with sewing curves, you may want to add more pins along the curve to hold the fabric in place while you sew.
>
> * Starching the fabric first helps you maintain control of the bias edges.

7. Keeping 1 on top, sew the curve with a ¼" seam. Press the seam toward 1. The block will measure 4½" square.

Sew.

8. Position the blocks, one row at a time. Sew the blocks in rows; then sew the rows together.

FINISHING

Layer, quilt, and bind (Layering and Basting, Quilting Ideas, and Binding, pages 9–13).

SOLACE FOR THE SCRAPLESS

notes

* Each fabric/letter should have prints all in the same color, but they do not need to be the exact same print.

* You will have some squares left over after cutting your fat quarters. With careful planning you can pull out some fabrics before they are cut so you end up with larger, rather than smaller, scraps.

Whirl in Prints, pieced and quilted by Emily Cier, 64" × 64"

For this version of *Whirl,* use yardage rather than scraps.

Stack the fat quarters from each colorway and cut 12 squares 5⅛" × 5⅛" from each fat quarter.

A: 3 fat quarters (need 34 squares)

B: 3 fat quarters (need 36 squares)

C: 4 fat quarters (need 45 squares)

D: 2 fat quarters (need 17 squares)

E: 3 fat quarters (need 31 squares)

F: 5 fat quarters (need 49 squares)

G: 4 fat quarters (need 48 squares)

Assemble by following Steps 2–8 on pages 47-49.

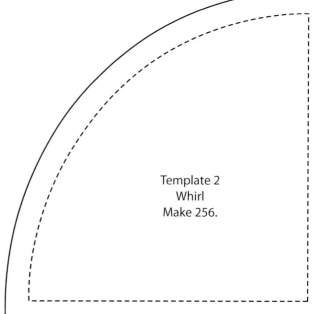

Template 2
Whirl
Make 256.

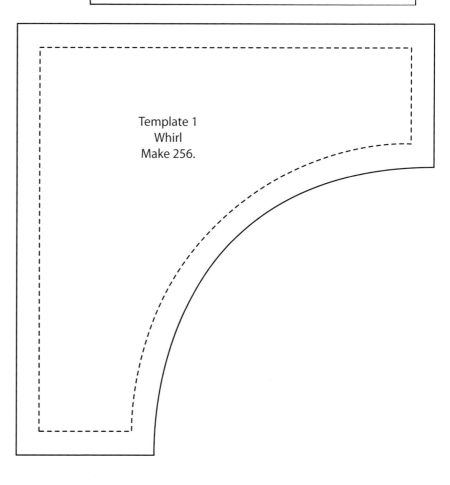

Template 1
Whirl
Make 256.

PIVOT

Pivot in Scraps, pieced by Emily Cier, quilted by Cathy Kirk, 60" × 60"

SCRAP SELECTION

This quilt is great for using up all the little white pieces lying around. Don't use too many large prints in the colored areas. Because so many colors touch, large prints will tend to make the shapes all blend together visually.

ASSEMBLY

Finished block size: 5″ × 10″

1. Piece the colored rectangles and white units to measure slightly larger than the dimensions shown. Make the quantities listed in Step 2. (The colors refer to the scrap colors in *Pivot in Scraps*; the letters (A)–(H) refer to the corresponding prints in *Pivot in Prints*.)

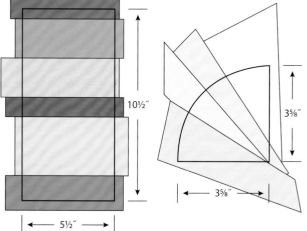

For alternate piecing designs, see Piecing Ideas (page 7).

2. Press and trim to sizes.

White (A): Cut 72 squares 3⅝″ × 3⅝″; then trim using Template 1.

Pink (B): Cut 6 rectangles 5½″ × 10½″.

Red (C): Cut 12 rectangles 5½″ × 10½″.

Orange (D): Cut 12 rectangles 5½″ × 10½″.

Yellow (E): Cut 12 rectangles 5½″ × 10½″.

Green (F): Cut 12 rectangles 5½″ × 10½″.

Blue (G): Cut 12 rectangles 5½″ × 10½″.

Purple (H): Cut 6 rectangles 5½″ × 10½″.

what you need

- White scraps (5″ × 1″–2″)

- Pink, red, orange, yellow, green, blue, and purple scraps (6″ wide × various lengths, 1″–2″ recommended)

- Backing: Pieced to 68″ × 68″ *or* 4 yards

- Batting: 68″ × 68″

- Binding: 2½″ wide × 260″ long, pieced from scraps; *or* ⅝ yard (cut into 7 strips)

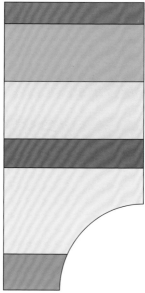

_____ *note*

The colors refer to the scrap colors in *Pivot in Scraps* and the letters (A)–(H) refer to the corresponding prints in *Pivot in Prints*.

3. Using Template 2, remove and discard the lower right corner of the rectangles.

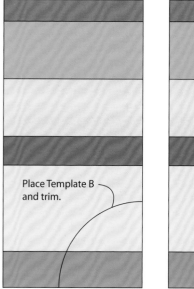

Place Template B and trim.

4. Take 1 colored rectangle and 1 white quarter-circle and place the right sides together with the rectangle on top. Align the centers and pin. Align the corners of the colored rectangle and the white quarter-circle on the left side and pin. Repeat on the right side. Keeping the rectangle on top, sew the curve with a ¼" seam. Press the seam toward the rectangle. (See *Whirl*, Steps 4-7, page 48, for more detailed instructions and illustrations on sewing this curve.)

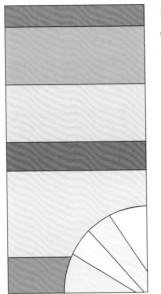

5. Following the diagram below, sew the rectangles and quarter-circles into rows; press and then sew the rows together.

FINISHING

Layer, quilt, and bind (Layering and Basting, Quilting Ideas, and Binding, pages 9–13)

SOLACE FOR THE SCRAPLESS

Each fabric/letter should have prints all in the same color, but they do not need to be the same print.

Cut 7 strips 3⅝" × width of fabric (wof); subcut into 72 squares 3⅝" × 3⅝". Trim to quarter-circles using Template 1.

B–H: Cut 1 strip from each print 5½" × wof; subcut each strip into 3 rectangles 5½" × 10½".

Proceed with Steps 2–5 on pages 52-53.

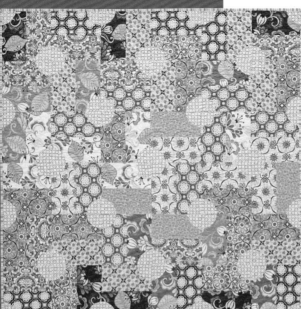

Pivot in Prints, pieced by Emily Cier, quilted by Cathy Kirk, 60" × 60"

For this version of *Pivot*, use yardage rather than scraps.

A: ⅞ yard for quarter-circles

B: 2 prints, ¼ yard each for rectangles

C: 4 prints, ¼ yard each for rectangles

D: 4 prints, ¼ yard each for rectangles

E: 4 prints, ¼ yard each for rectangles

F: 4 prints, ¼ yard each for rectangles

G: 4 prints, ¼ yard each for rectangles

H: 2 prints, ¼ yard each for rectangles

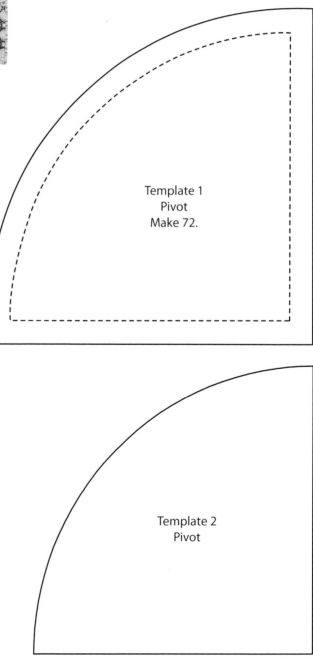

Template 1
Pivot
Make 72.

Template 2
Pivot

ABOUT
the Author

Emily Cier has had a lifelong love of fine art and art history and has a background in graphic design. These passions finally found common ground in quilting, which she quickly discovered to be a wonderful and timeless creative outlet as well as one filled with a rich history. It also keeps one quite toasty on a cold, rainy day.

Emily lives in Seattle with her husband and two beautiful children (who are showing their own penchant for creativity).

Also by Emily Cier

Great Titles *from* C&T PUBLISHING & STASH BOOKS

Available at your local retailer or **www.ctpub.com** *or* **800-284-1114**

For a list of other fine books from C&T Publishing, visit our website
to view our catalog online.

C&T PUBLISHING, INC.

P.O. Box 1456
Lafayette, CA 94549
800-284-1114

Email: ctinfo@ctpub.com
Website: www.ctpub.com

C&T Publishing's professional photography services are now available to
the public. Visit us at www.ctmediaservices.com.

Tips and Techniques can be found at www.ctpub.com > Consumer
Resources > Quiltmaking Basics: Tips & Techniques for Quiltmaking & More

For quilting supplies:

COTTON PATCH

1025 Brown Ave.
Lafayette, CA 94549
Store: 925-284-1177
Mail order: 925-283-7883

Email: CottonPa@aol.com
Website: www.quiltusa.com

Note: Fabrics used in the quilts shown may not be currently
available, as fabric manufacturers keep most fabrics in print for
only a short time.